ANIMALS &ME

Dolphins and Me

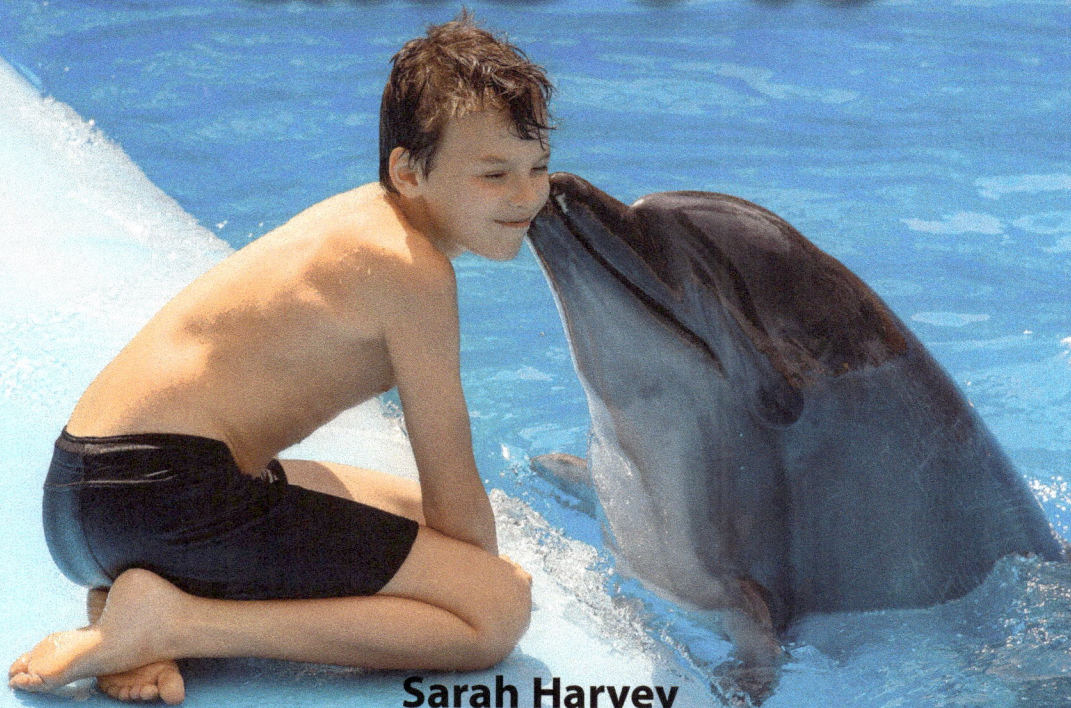

Sarah Harvey

Explore other books at:
WWW.ENGAGEBOOKS.COM

VANCOUVER, B.C.

www.ENGAGEBOOKS.COM

Dolphins and Me
Animals and Me
Harvey, Sarah N., 1950 –
Edited by: A.R. Roumanis
Text © 2022 Engage Books
Design © 2022 Engage Books

Text set in GelPenUpright

FIRST EDITION / FIRST PRINTING

LIBRARY AND ARCHIVES CANADA CATALOGUING IN PUBLICATION

Title: Dolphins and me / by Sarah Harvey
Names: Harvey, Sarah N., 1950- author
Description: Series statement: Animals and me

Identifiers: Canadiana (print) 20220395403 | Canadiana (ebook) 20220395411
ISBN 978-1-77476-688-0 (hardcover)
ISBN 978-1-77476-689-7 (softcover)
ISBN 978-1-77476-690-3 (epub)
ISBN 978-1-77476-691-0 (pdf)

Subjects:
LCSH: Dolphins—Juvenile literature.
LCSH: Dolphins—Behavior—Juvenile literature.
LCSH: Human behavior—Juvenile literature.

Classification: LCC QL737.C432 H37 2022 | DDC J599.53—DC23

This project has been made possible in part
by the Government of Canada.

Canada

What do you know about dolphins?

Dolphins live in every ocean of the world.

Do you live near the ocean?

5

Dolphins are not fish.
They are marine mammals.

They need to
breathe air to live.

6

Is a dog a mammal?
Are you?

Baby dolphins are called calves.

What other animal baby is called a calf?

Dolphins live in
groups called pods.

Who lives in your pod?

11

The largest dolphin is the orca, which can weigh over 10,000 pounds.

That's almost three times as heavy as a car!

13

Large pods of orcas can span four generations, from babies to great-grandparents.

How many generations are there in your family?

Dolphins talk by using squeaks, clicks and whistles.

Can you whistle?

17

Dolphins can have up to 200 sharp teeth.

How many teeth do you have? Are any of them sharp?

Narwhals are dolphins too. They only have two teeth. Some narwhals grow one long tooth called a tusk.

How would you eat if you only had two teeth?

Dolphins have a hole in the top of their heads called a blowhole. They use it to breathe.

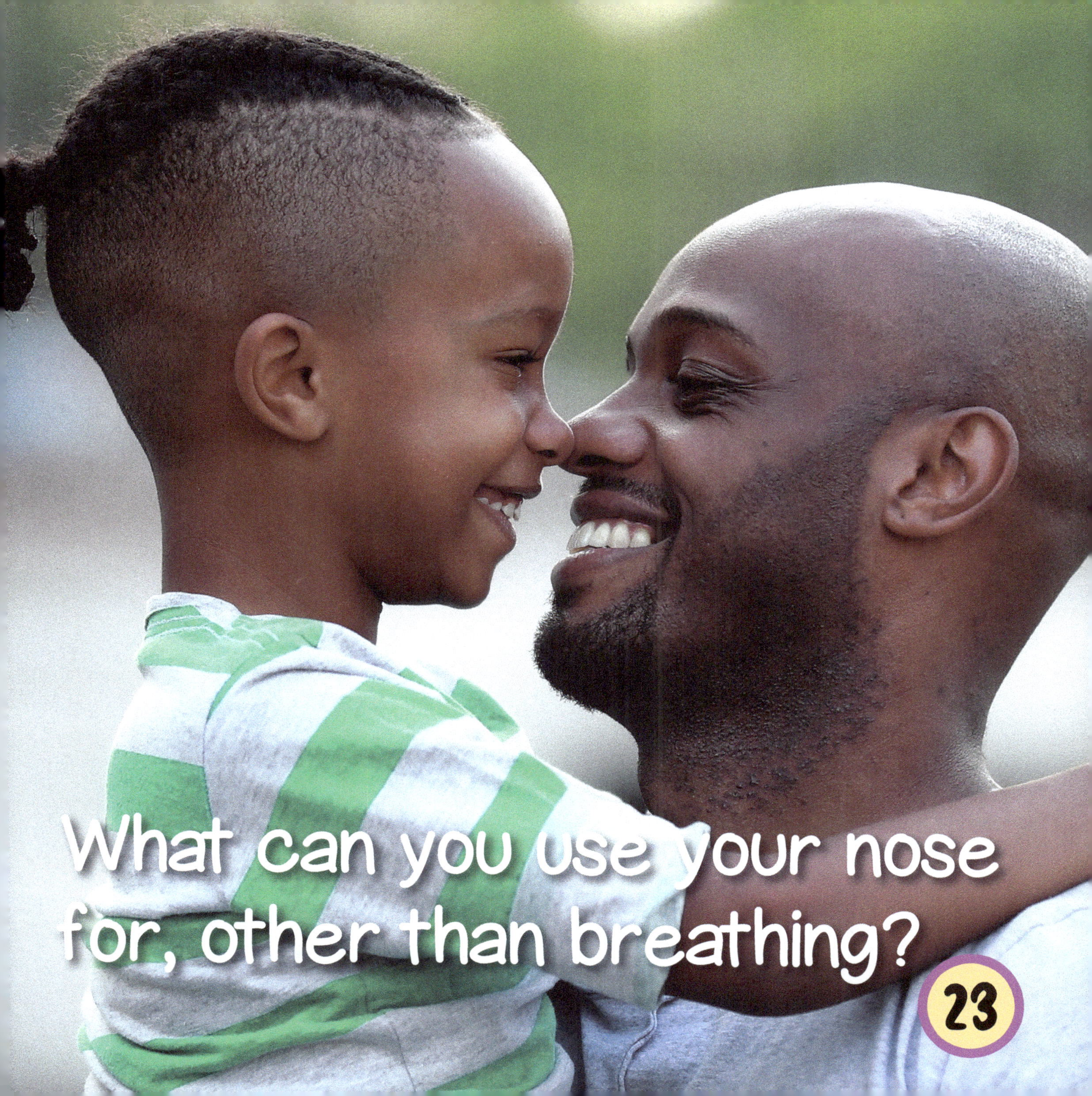

What can you use your nose for, other than breathing?

Dolphins can jump 20 feet out of the water.

How high can you jump?

25

Dolphins can see really well underwater and out of the water.

Do you keep your eyes open or shut underwater?

The smallest dolphin is the Hector's dolphin, which only weighs about 100 pounds.

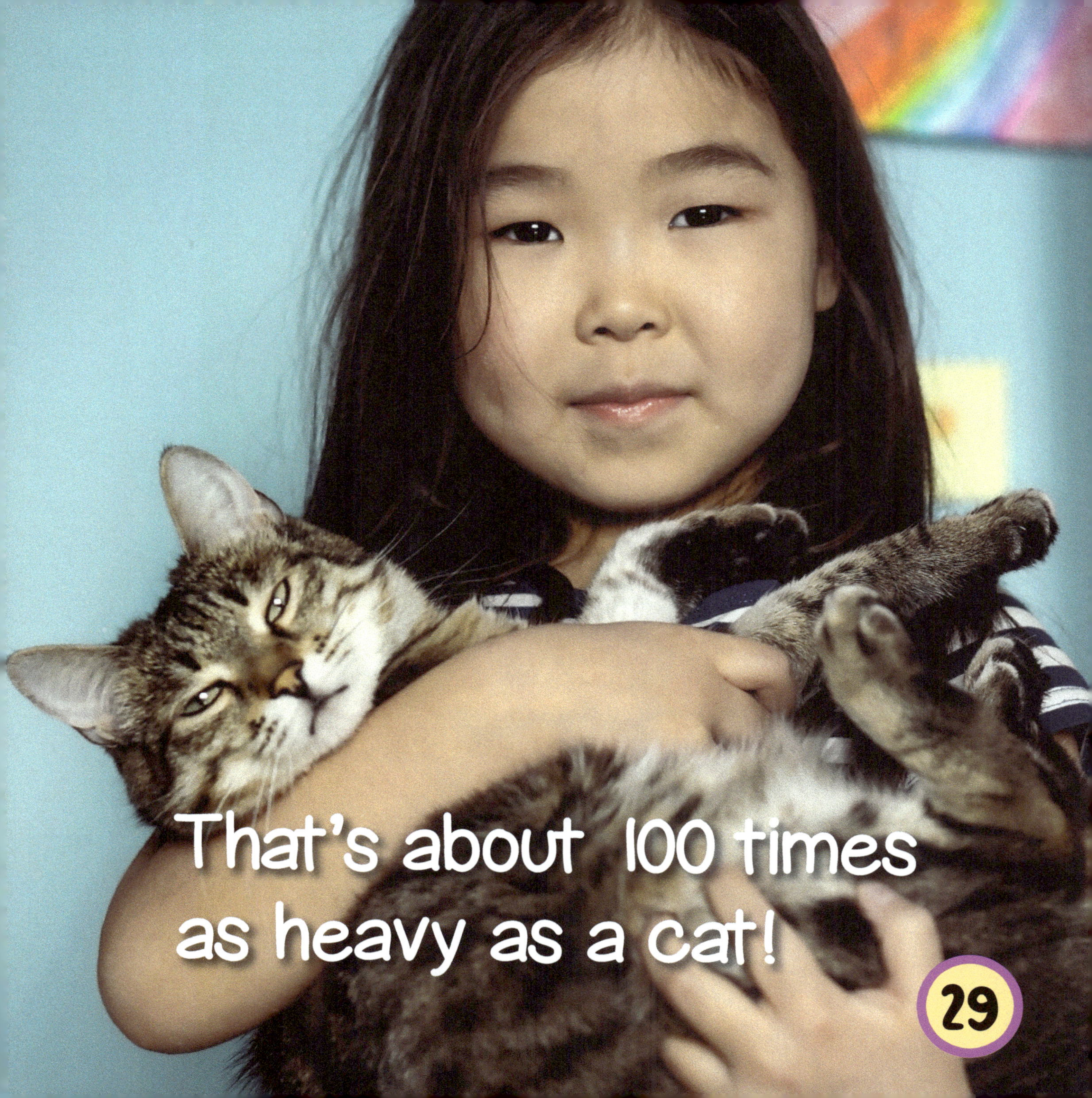

That's about 100 times
as heavy as a cat!

Bottlenose dolphins often look as if they are smiling.

What makes you smile?

31

www.ingramcontent.com/pod-product-compliance
Lightning Source LLC
Chambersburg PA
CBHW041435040426

42452CB00023B/2980